Young, Wild & Free

A 31 Day Devotional Inspiring Growth
and Fulfillment for College Women

Apris Howey

_____

Presented To

_____

By

_____

Date

Young, Wild & Free

Copyright © 2019 by Apris Howey

Graphic design by Xavier Freeman (instagram.com/xayfree)

Editorial services by Emily Stains

Printed in the United States of America

ISBN:9781794374621

I dedicate this book to the young woman that is on a wild chase after her true self and calling. I dedicate this book to the young woman that is also unashamed, bold, and fearless in her walk. May you continue to seek and find all of what you need and more. My heart's desire is that you will have a new-found freedom in your identity and that God will reveal himself to you in a new and mighty way. Your college years will be the start of something fresh and new. This is only the beginning.

Table of Contents

Introduction

I want to share with you all a bit about the woman behind the vision. The one who found herself in the midst of an identity-crisis. My junior year of college was a pivotal moment in my life. I would say it was the time I had my first real encounter with God. It was the year I made the best decision of my life, to begin my journey following Christ. Throughout my life I grew up in church and was always involved whether it was youth ministry, singing in the choir, dance ministry, outreach, etc. I've had many experiences with God, but none like this one. This was something different, something new and re-found.

I came into college anxious like most people. I was anxious of what it would be like and if it would live up to my expectations. I had so many unanswered questions in the back of my mind. The last thing I was thinking about was God, purpose, and my future. I was more concerned with living out the "college experience" to the fullest. I made some friends and lost some friends. I made some mistakes and allowed myself to get distracted and be consumed by alcohol, drugs, boys and my own insecurities. I allowed these things to temporarily fill a void, not recognizing that they were only supplements to the fulfillment that was waiting for me in Christ. It is a lot easier to "fake it until you make it" rather than admitting something is wrong on the inside of you. That would mean I'd have to face myself, take a look in the mirror, and do serious heart work.

Although I came in that way, I didn't leave the same. Somewhere along the journey I let God begin the heart reparation inside of me. I chose the narrative that was written about me, the narrative of grace, love, mercy and forgiveness. The problem wasn't solely about my actions and decisions, but essentially the reasoning behind them.

Sometimes we get so consumed by our mess that we don't even realize we are in the midst of losing ourselves. Choose to accept the love of God. There is nothing that can separate us from it. It continuously transforms and molds us. By choosing God we choose ourselves, and that is the best choice that we could will ever make.

The purpose behind this devotional is to invoke you to a certain level of growth and fulfillment. We are going to challenge and disrupt the world's definition of what it means to be "young, wild and free". We are no longer accepting the stigma of the "college girl". You are more than what society portrays you to be. You get to decide which narrative you will believe. Truth is, you don't have to wait to be great. You don't have to wait to be noticed. And you definitely don't have to wait to be understood. It is time to be empowered and get excited about what God is doing, and how He wants to use you now!

The true definition of being young, wild and free has less to do about satisfaction that comes from temporary people, places and things; and more to do about fulfillment in Christ. When I think about what it means to be "young, wild and free," I am reminded of this quote: "Be fearless in the pursuit of what sets your soul on fire". There is freedom in being who God called you to be, and not letting other people's opinions deter you from what you believe. Let nothing and no one get in the way of your pursuit of God. There are promises in the pursuit, and there is passion and purpose in the pursuit. Don't let you fears into your heart and steal what God has in store for you. Choose to pursue wholeheartedly and be young, wild and free.

Throughout my journey of writing this devotional I have laughed, cried and just about everything in between. I like to go for a run or workout whenever I feel overly-stressed and anxious. On this particular day I was running along the sidewalk in my neighborhood and I saw a couple of wildflowers growing in between the grass and the concrete. The flowers that I found were the same flowers that inspired the message and vision behind me writing this devotional. I knew it was a sign of hope from God and that He was confirming the great work He established inside of me. My prayer is that like the wildflower you bloom despite your circumstances and despite the conditions around you, that you will be rooted and grounded in something concrete, that you will have evidence, through your faith, of the God that lives inside of you.

Each devotional will consist of a daily read, meditation on the Word, thought provoking questions, and then are sealed by prayer and words of affirmation. My vision was for this devotional to be a book of hope, love, and empowerment. My heart's desire is that each day these words will renew your passion, draw you closer to God's love and empower you to fulfill your purpose. I am excited that God has allowed us to embark on this journey of growth and fulfillment together, and that my purpose is connected you and yours. Let's get to work!

Day 1

Ready, Set, Go!

The time is now. Stop waiting for the perfect place, the perfect moment, the perfect time to dedicate your life to Christ. You might say to yourself, "Maybe in five years I'll have my stuff together" or "I'm not ready for that just yet". You might even be afraid of what you'll have to give up or what you think you'll miss. You might even think that what you're doing is "good enough" or having a relationship with Christ is something that only "weird" religious people have. That type of mindset is robbing you from the greatest thing you could ever experience.

Many people say that your college years are supposed to be some of your best years. I couldn't agree with that statement more. My college years were some of my best years because they were the time that I found myself in finding Christ. College is the place where I found my purpose, my identity, and the people that would help take me to the next level. I was young, but I was powerful, as are you. God wants to do a similar thing in your life. He wants to meet you where you are and transform you into the best version of yourself. He wants you to rely on Him, like you never have before. He wants you to be an example for others, where they see Christ when they look at you. There is true beauty and power in having a relationship with God during this season of your life. Get ready, because God is about to set you in places you thought you would never go.

Meditate on these scriptures:

- ○ "Let no one despise you for your youth, but set the believers an example in speech, in conduct, in love, in faith, in purity." (1 Timothy 4:12) ESV
- ○ "How can a young person stay pure? By obeying your word." (Psalm 119:9) NLT

Reflection:

o If it isn't your age, what do you think is hindering your commitment to God?

_____

_____

_____

_____

_____

Prayer:

Father,

I want to grow in my relationship with you. I want to commit my life to you. I thank you for loving and trusting me enough to be an example for other believers and for allowing Jesus to be the perfect example for me. I pray that you will continue to bless me, keep me, and guide me throughout my college journey. I need you more than ever and I know that you are here with me. I pray that I will turn to you, not just in a time of trouble or need, but at all times, and that I wouldn't result in worldly coping methods. Send the right people at the right timing that are meant to be a part of my journey. I thank you for placing me here and for your plan for my life. I can't wait to see all you have planned for me. In Jesus' name, Amen.

Affirmations:

- I am young, and I am powerful.

Day 2

"Something Told Me"

If you are going to move forward with the intent to bring God into your everyday life, there is one thing you need to understand. Something never told you anything. The something told me phenomenon is a way of discrediting Holy Spirit's interaction and presence in our daily lives. Holy Spirit is constantly leading and guiding us to make the right moves and decisions. Some people may call it intuition, others may call it a "gut feeling". We are constantly being directed, even when we don't realize it.

Holy Spirit knows all things, and the deep things of God. Therefore, we have to be submitted to Holy Spirit in order to embrace the fullness of God. You may be wondering, "What does this mean?" or "What does this look like?". This means that when you feel an inclination to do something, you do it. Making a habit out of this will help strengthen your trust in Holy Spirit. Our obedience doesn't only affect our own destiny, but it interferes with what God is doing in other people's lives. Imagine it was placed on your heart to give a student in your class money, but you decided not to because you only had a $20 bill and didn't want to give away that much money. In actuality, $20 was exactly what that student needed to buy a book they couldn't afford. Now imagine if you were that student. Move out of the way and let Holy Spirit work through you. Attempting to navigate college without His guidance will cause you to miss the power of God.

Meditate on these scriptures:

○ "But the Helper, the Holy Spirit, whom the Father will send in my name, he will teach you all things and bring to your remembrance all that I have said to you." (John 14:26) ESV o "And the Spirit of the Lord shall rest upon him, the Spirit of wisdom and understanding, the Spirit of counsel and might, the Spirit of knowledge and the fear of the Lord." (Isaiah 11:2) ESV

Reflection:

o Think about a time the Holy Spirit was moving you to do something. Did you do it? Why or why not?

Prayer:

Father,

Thank you for sending us your spirit. I am open to the guidance and direction of Holy Spirit in my daily life. I want my actions and decisions to be made out of wisdom, knowledge and understanding. I no longer want to live void and out of agreement with your spirit. Renew a right mind and spirit within me. In Jesus' name I pray, Amen.

Affirmations:

- I will no longer refer to Holy Spirit as "something."

Day 3

Loved

You are loved. You need to internalize this. No mistake or wrongdoing could ever separate you from God's love. There is no need to feel guilt, shame, or self-hatred for the things that you have done. Those are tactics to keep you from discovering the truth in who you really are and God's unwavering love for you. The Father showed the greatest act of love when He sent His Son Jesus to die on the cross for us. It was love that brought Jesus to the cross, and love that kept Him there until death.

The word of God teaches and shows us that God is love (1 John 4:8). It is impossible to know love, without having a love relationship. Your relationship with God will set the standard for your relationships with other people. The love that you have for yourself should be a representation of the love God has always had for you. You are a daughter of a King and you are loved beyond measures. After you have experienced a love encounter with God, your life will never be the same again. The love of God has the power to change/shift the direction of things and intercede on your behalf. That's just what happened after Jesus died on the cross. God already called us chosen and loved. It's up to us to believe that about ourselves. Embrace the love God has for you, because without it you wouldn't be standing. In a world that determines worth by temporary likes and followers, our God has a permanent and relentless love for us.

Meditate on these scriptures:

- ○ "But God shows his love for us in that while we were still sinners, Christ died for us." (Romans 5:8) ESV
- ○ "Who shall separate us from the love of Christ? Shall tribulation, or distress, or

persecution, or famine, or nakedness, or danger, or sword? As it is written, "For your sake we are being killed all the day long; we are regarded as sheep to be slaughtered." No, in all these things we are more than conquerors through him who loved us. For I am sure that neither death nor life, nor angels nor rulers, nor things present nor things to come, nor powers, nor height nor depth, nor anything else in all creation, will be able to separate us from the love of God in Christ Jesus our Lord." (Romans 8:35-39) ESV

Reflection:

o Do you ever find it difficult to love yourself? How can you better demonstrate the love of God to yourself and others?

_____

_____

_____

_____

_____

Prayer:

Father,

I thank you for being the definition of love. Help me to love myself and others in the manner that You do. I want to have a love encounter with You that will change the way I view myself. Thank you for loving me when I didn't love myself and for continually showing me Your grace and favor. As I grower closer to you I want to experience and embrace the fullness of Your love, even if I may not always understand it. I am grateful for the sacrifice of Jesus so that I could be forgiven and live a life of freedom and love. In Jesus' name, Amen.

Affirmations :

○   I am forever forgiven and loved.

Day 4

Beauty and Brains

I love this quote by Audrey Hepburn: "True beauty in a woman is reflected in her soul." A woman of God is more than just a pretty face. She has far more to offer than make-up, heels, and the latest Fashion Nova fit. Don't be so focused on the outside that you forget about the inside. Despite how the world depicts us as women, we seek our validation and identity from the Word of God; or at least we should. The confusion occurs when we openly accept what society says about us. Never shrink yourself to fit in someone else's box. God never designed you to be in a box, He created you to think, thrive, and function outside of one.

You are a creative being that was hand-crafted to do amazing work in the Kingdom of God. You are clothed in strength and dignity (Proverbs 31:25). Fill your mind and spirit with the affirmations of God and you will transform from the inside out. Allow your inner-beauty and intelligence to captivate the hearts of others. In return, it will help lead them to Christ. As a college student it can be easy to get wrapped up in a false-identity. If you are ever feeling unappreciated, uneducated, or unworthy, refer to His Word. Allow the scriptures below to minister to you heart. They will help you develop a deeper understanding of who you are as a woman of God.

Meditate on these scriptures:

o "I praise you, for I am fearfully and wonderfully made. Wonderful are your works; my soul knows it very well." (Psalm: 139:14) ESV

o Charm is deceptive, and beauty does not last; but a woman who fears the LORD will be greatly praised. (Proverbs 31:30) NLT

- "The fear of the LORD is the beginning of wisdom, and the knowledge of the Holy One is insight." (Proverbs 9:10) ESV

Reflection:

- What makes you beautiful to the Lord?

Prayer :

Father,

I thank you for creating me in the manner that You did. Not only did you hand-craft me, but you designed me with beauty, love and creativity. I thank you for giving me identity as a woman of God. I pray that I accept the truths about me and turn away from the lies. I am excited to learn more about myself and the ways I can reflect my inner-beauty, which comes from You. I pray that I will turn to You in the times that I feel uncertain about myself and my capabilities. I hope to gain more wisdom and knowledge as I dig deeper into Your Word. In Jesus name, Amen.

Affirmations :

- ○ I am fearfully and wonderfully made.

Day 5

Freedom

There is a certain level of freedom that needs to be attained in order for you to discover and walk out your purpose. True freedom comes from Christ (John 8:36). Understanding your freedom in Christ will change your outlook on life and the people that surround you. God affirms and accepts you, therefore no one else can deny you. You are free from the opinions and judgements of people. Freedom doesn't mean that people won't talk about you or try to discourage you from your dreams. It doesn't mean that there won't be any challenges and obstacles. It simply means that you are not bound by life circumstances and the opinions of man.

Your freedom gives you the confidence you walk out your God-given purpose. It fuels you with hope when the world gives you disappointment. It keeps you in right alignment with your destiny, despite what is going on around you. People are attracted to those who demonstrate the freedom and love of Christ. It is contagious. Walk in your freedom. Walk in your calling. Walk in your destiny. Stop waiting on someone else to notice, validate and accept you. Christ died for you to walk in freedom. Be the woman of God that you are called to be today!

Meditate on these scriptures :

- ○ "Now the Lord is the Spirit, and where the Spirit of the Lord is, there is freedom." (2 Corinthians 3:17) NIV
- ○ "For you have been called to live in freedom, my brothers and sisters. But don't use your freedom to satisfy your sinful nature. Instead, use your freedom to serve one another in love." (Galatians 5:13) NLT
- ○ "In him and through faith in him we may approach God with freedom and confidence." (Ephesians 3:12) NIV

Reflection:

○ What does true freedom in Christ look like to you? How can you embrace it?

_____

_____

_____

_____

_____

Prayer:

Father,

I thank you for giving me freedom and authority. I never want to live a life of bondage. I want to experience true freedom that comes from Christ. I speak freedom over my life in my actions, my decisions, and my purpose. I will no longer seek affirmation and acceptance from another source. You are the source of my freedom and joy. In Jesus name, Amen.

Affirmations:

o   I am free in Christ.

Day 6

Priorities

So, I have to ask this question. How do your priorities look? What is the first thing that you do or think about when you wake up in the morning? Do you tend to set your dreams and passions on the backburner? What is more important to you, your agenda or God's agenda? I wish I would have learned the importance of placing God at the top of my priority list when I first started college. It wasn't until my senior year that I actually started serving the Lord and committing myself to the plan that He had for my life. I started my freshman year with a 4.0 GPA and each semester it went down. After the spring semester of my junior year, my GPA dropped just below a 3.1.

The fall semester of my senior year was probably the busiest semester I ever had. I was traveling once a month to train in Atlanta for acting and modeling, a calling God revealed to me earlier that year. I was singing on the praise team at my church, Surge, as well as attending weekly practices, going to bible study/prayer on two college campuses and going to bible study/prayer at Surge. I was also working once a week with a local acting production company for kids. I practiced praying, reading the word, and listening to worship music in the morning/throughout the day. On top of this, I had a senior course load which consisted of mainly senior level courses. Despite all of this, this was the first time my GPA increased since I came to college and it rose back to a 3.1. I say all of this to say that when you are in right alignment with God's will and purpose for your life, He will provide for you. You will never regret making God a priority in your life.

Meditate on these scriptures:

o "Seek the Kingdom of God above all else, and live righteously, and he will give you everything you need." (Matthew 6:33) NLT

o "Commit your actions to the LORD, and your plans will succeed." (Proverbs 16:3) NLT

o "The Lord directs the steps of the godly. He delights in every detail of their lives." (Psalm 37:23) NLT

Reflection:

o Consider what ways your life will change once you get your priorities in order.

Prayer:

Father,

There is nothing or no one in this world that is more important than you. I thank you for showing me the importance of making You the number one priority in my life. I want to commit my actions and will to You. Help me to seek Your Kingdom above all other things. I pray that Your will be done in my life and that I come into agreement with it. Use me God, on my campus and in the surrounding community. I want to serve You like I never have before. In Jesus name, Amen.

Affirmations:

- God is my number one priority.

Day 7

"Make it Plain"

God communicates with us in unique ways. Many of His plans are revealed to us in glimpses of the future or creative thoughts and ideas. As you are growing closer to Him, you should practice writing down your dreams, visions, goals, aspirations, and everything you feel is necessary to accomplish God's will for your life. This keeps God's promises close to your mind and heart. My hope is that as you are reading this devotional, God will begin to pour into you like never before. In moments like this, journal every thought and insight that is revealed to you. Trust me, you don't want to make the same mistake I did, missing vital information that God was pouring into me through different people, but I didn't think to write it down and make it plain. Now, I'm learning my lesson.

God is constantly speaking to us. Once you develop a greater understanding of how He communicates, this will become clearer to you. You will become more confident in your vision because you know it is from God, and no one else can tell you otherwise. During times of frustration, journaling will be especially helpful to you. It allows you to release your emotions on pen and paper but refer to the truths God already revealed to you. In those moments you will find a sense of serenity and comfort from the words you've written. If you don't already, I challenge you today to find a journal, buy a notebook, open a word document and begin to write. Type, draw, do whatever you have to do; just make it visible. Let your thoughts flow, and let the Holy Spirit speak to you.

Meditate on these scriptures :

○ "Then the Lord told me: "I will give you my message in the form of a vision. Write it clearly enough to be read at a glance. At the time I have decided, my words will come true. You can trust what I say about the future. It may take a long time, but keep on waiting— it will happen!" (Habakkuk 2: 2-3) CEV

o "The plans of the diligent lead surely to abundance and advantage, But everyone who acts in haste comes surely to poverty." (Proverbs 21:5) AMP

Reflection:

o Have you written down the vision/plan God gave you for your life? (If not, do so. If you are unaware of what that vision is, continue to ask in prayer until you do.)

Prayer:

Father,

I ask that you reveal Your vision and will for my life so that I can make it plain. I trust in Your plan and I pray that I won't grow weary in doing good, because at Your appointed time I will reap a harvest. I thank You for placing me here in college where I can grow and learn more about myself and You. Help me to form the habit of writing down all of the things You show me, so I can refer to them when I become discouraged. I speak that You will pour out to me through visions and signs, and that they will be clear to me. In Jesus name, Amen.

Affirmations:

○   I will seek and trust God for His visions.

Day 8

Heart to Serve

A heart to serve stems from giving your life to Christ and the daily pursuit to be more like Him. And by giving your life to Christ, I don't just mean accepting Him as Your Lord and Savior, I mean accepting Him daily and choosing to follow the path He set before you. In order to become more like Christ, we have to understand His characteristics and why He did what He did while He was here on Earth. Everything about Christ was selfless, He was sent here to serve and so were we. He is the perfect model for how we should be living our lives and letting the Father use us for the benefit of others. With that being said, I want you to think about the ways you could better demonstrate the selfless nature of Christ.

We could all be more kind, more giving and less selfish, but it is the pureness of our hearts that distinguishes us as believers. Our heart to serve is a reflection of our love for the Lord. We serve God, because we love Him and because He first loved us. It is a privilege and honor for us to serve the Most-High God. We should all be involved in the work of the Lord. Serve at a local church, volunteer at a community center, get involved in organizations on your campus, apply to become a residential assistant (RA), or join a campus ministry. Serve through your gifts, your purpose, your time and your talents. Your campus is a great place to start. God's people are everywhere and could use a servant's heart like yours. Take the work of the Lord seriously, it is your sole purpose for being here, and you will surely be rewarded for it.

Meditate on these scriptures:

○ "Work willingly at whatever you do, as though you were working for the Lord rather than for people. Remember that the Lord will give you an inheritance as your reward, and that the Master you are serving is Christ." (Colossians 3:23-24) NLT

o "For even the Son of Man came not to be served but to serve, and to give his life as a ransom for many." (Mark 10:45) ESV

o "Do nothing from selfish ambition or conceit, but in humility count others more significant than yourselves. Let each of you look not only to his own interests, but also to the interests of others." (Philippians 2:3-4) ESV

Reflection:

o Do you carry the heart to serve? If not, how can you harvest it?

_____

_____

_____

_____

_____

Prayer:

Father,

Purify my heart and create a longing to serve You. Teach me how to be selfless so that I can serve in a way that is acceptable to You and that is Christ-like. Lead me to the people and places where I am called to serve and be a blessing to. I pray that you will use me and allow me to be an example to others on how to serve You with the right mind, heart and spirit. In Jesus name, Amen.

Affirmations:

o I will serve the Lord.

Day 9

"Godfidence"

"I can do all things through Christ who strengthens me." (Philippians 4:13)

Philippians 4:13 sets the tone for today's devotional. Start by meditating on it. What does it mean? What does it look like to you? You may be thinking, "Can I really do all things through Christ?". The answer is yes. God is not a liar; His Word is true (Numbers 23:19). So, what does this mean for us? It means that we have to go from a place of reading the Word, to understanding the Word, to living out the Word. I'm sure many people have heard this scripture before, but they haven't internalized it to the point of trying something new. Allow this scripture to truly speak to your heart. It will change your outlook on a lot of things, especially your purpose and your relationship with Christ.

Your confidence in self derives from your confidence in God. This is what I like to call "Godfidence". Your Godfidence is going to take you to the next level. It will enable you to see the fruit in your life that comes from diligence, hard work, and trust in God. Without Godfidence, you will never be able to accomplish any God-given dream, purpose, or vision. Our lack of confidence in ourselves and/or in God is what usually hinders us from reaching our fullest potential, where we live and thrive under the glory of God. Chose Godfidence over doubt and insecurity. God did not create you to lack in confidence and boldness. He did not create you to half-way be great. The people of God have always been radical and done miraculous things. Now it's your turn.

Meditate on these scriptures:

○ "But blessed is the one who trusts in the LORD, whose confidence is in him." (Jeremiah 17:7) NIV o "So, let us come boldly to the throne of our gracious God. There we will receive his mercy, and we will find grace to help us when we need it most." (Hebrews 4:16) NLT

Reflection :

o What is hindering you from achieving greatness and relying on the power of God?

_____

_____

_____

_____

_____

Prayer:

Father,

Thank You for allowing me to come to Your throne boldly and with confidence. I want to fully rely on Your strength and power, and not my own capabilities. I know that my strength and confidence come from You, and Your strength is made perfect in my weakness. I am grateful to serve a God that helps me achieve greatness and created me to be bold as a lion. Through You I can do all things. In Jesus name, Amen.

Affirmations :

- ○ I can do ALL things through Christ who strengthens me.
- ○ I am a bold, confident and strong woman.

Day 10

Self – Care

Self-care is a form of self-love. I can't express enough how important it is to take care of your body, especially while in college. Your body, mind, and emotions are all connected. Therefore, in order for you to function at your maximum potential, you need to practice being in good health. Good health may look different to certain types of people, but there is one thing that we can agree on: everyone looks and feels better when they are properly taking care of themselves. By creating a lifestyle than includes regular exercise, you can help improve your memory and thinking capability. Wouldn't we all benefit from that?

I didn't develop the habit of working out and taking care of my body until my junior year of college. I made some minor lifestyle adjustments that changed my life. It was the decision to lose my old-self in order to gain the woman I was to become. Either way you are going to lose something. About a year after that, I had lost 30 pounds. I share this story SIMPLY for motivation and my prayer is that someone will read it and take the steps to change their life. My last question for you is what are you eating? Trust me I get it, food is good. I love to cook, and I love to eat, but are you using food as a supplement for stress, anxiety, or sadness? If you are, we pray against that in the name of Jesus and that you would find healthier ways to release. The food you eat is meant to work for you, not against you. God is the ultimate Healer, but He created food to help nourish our bodies and give us the proper nutrients we need to be fruitful and multiply. Take care of your temple, and of course indulge every now and then. That's a part of self-care too.

Meditate on these scriptures:

o "Or do you not know that your body is a temple of the Holy Spirit within you, whom you have from God? You are not your own, for you were bought with a price. So, glorify God in your body." (1 Corinthians 6:19-20) ESV

o "Beloved, I pray that in every way you may succeed and prosper and be in good health [physically], just as [I know] your soul prospers [spiritually]." (3 John 1:2) AMP

Reflection :

o What are some lifestyle adjustments I need to make to take care of my body?

_____

_____

_____

_____

_____

Prayer:

Father,

Help me to take care of my body so that I can be in good health. Give me the wisdom and understanding to make better decisions surrounding my body and health. I want to live a long and plentiful life. I pray against using food as a source of release. You are the true Source of my peace, comfort, relief, and joy. Allow me to worship you through my body and living a life that is healthy and pleasing to you. In Jesus name, Amen.

Affirmations:

o   I will live a healthy and plentiful life.

Day 11

Girls Just Wanna Have Fun

Don't fall for the trap. I went into college with the mindset that I had to prove myself. I wanted to enjoy the fullness of the so called "college-experience." In high school I was always different. I knew I wasn't the same, but I somewhat wanted to be. Many people experience these same emotions, but they don't speak on them. Instead they choose to settle for the easy route, "sticking to the norm." This is because we are not taught how to respond to the pull of God. When I first came to college it was easier for me to be like everybody else than to be who I truly was, especially when being who I was wasn't always accepted.

The truth of the matter is this: you don't have to prove anything to anyone, it is not a competition. If you seek validation from this world and other people you will constantly feel rejected and unworthy. If you try to numb the pain and truth through drugs, alcohol, partying, and guys you will grow to dislike yourself. You may even begin to enjoy the temporary fulfillment, but it is TEMPORARY. I've had my fair share of these things, but I can assure you they will leave you feeling empty. Sometimes we don't even recognize that is what we are doing. There is a better way for you to deal with "it," whatever that "it" is. Face it dead on. Don't run. Don't deny. Don't hide. Your Father wants you to be free. He wants you to confide in Him. He wants to renew your mind and establish a new way of thinking in you. He sees you not by your mistakes, but by your heart and the precious daughter you are to Him. There is love, freedom, and acceptance in Him. Choose that over anything else.

Meditate on these scriptures:

o "Don't copy the behavior and customs of this world, but let God transform you into a new person by changing the way you think. Then you will learn to know God's will for you, which is good and pleasing and perfect." (Romans 12:2) NLT

o "Don't become so well-adjusted to your culture that you fit into it without even thinking. Instead, fix your attention on God. You'll be changed from the inside out. Readily recognize what he wants from you, and quickly respond to it. Unlike the culture around you, always dragging you down to its level of immaturity, God brings the best out of you, develops well-formed maturity in you." (Romans 12:2,) MSG

Reflection:

o Consider some fun ways you can get involved on your campus and enjoy your college-experience. Be creative.

Prayer:

Father,

I give it to you, all of the hurt, pain, and mistakes. Transform me in my mind and my thoughts. I want to exemplify the mind and heart of Christ. I pray that I have a fun, exciting and memorable college experience that aligns with Your perfect will for my life. Allow me to set an example in faith and in purity for other believers and students on my campus. Teach me how to be more Christ-like in my words, actions, decisions, and the way I carry myself. Thank you accepting and loving me for who I am. In Jesus name, Amen.

Affirmations:

o   I am accepted and renewed.

Day 12

Living Your Best Life

"When the desires of you heart meet God's purpose for your life, that is living your best life."

This quote was the perfect way to begin today's devotional. There is a common misconception going around called "living your best life". No matter how great your life may be, God always has greater in store for those who love Him. Don't accept what is permissible when you can live under the perfect will of God. Living your best life is never wasting your time, nor is it living desolate of your purpose. In order for us to live our best lives, we have to look to the Word of God to see how we should be living our lives. You'd be surprised to find that the way to live is not just about us and what we want. It is much about how God wants to use us and how we should treat each other.

Your purpose is for other people, just as it is for you. When you are submitted to God you find joy in the work of the Lord and showing love to His people. It is a desire of your heart to fulfill the will of God. Your passion for your purpose and the things that you love grows stronger. Once I came into agreement with these things, I began to connect the dots in my life. I could see how God used the desires He placed in my heart to align with my purpose, and it is one of the greatest feelings. Your purpose is greatly influenced by the way you treat others. Whatever is in your heart will flow out of it. You want to produce good fruit, that will last and reproduce. People will remember the encounters you had with them over anything else. Just imagine how much greater your life would be, living it the best way possible.

Meditate on these scriptures:

- "Delight yourself in the LORD, and he will give you the desires of your heart." (Psalm 37:4) ESV
- "You did not choose me, but I chose you and appointed you that you should go and bear fruit and that your fruit should abide, so that whatever you ask the Father in my name, he may give it to you." (John 15:16) ESV
- "We ask God to give you complete knowledge of his will and to give you spiritual wisdom and understanding. Then the way you live will always honor and please the Lord, and your lives will produce every kind of good fruit. All the while, you will grow as you learn to know God better and better." (Colossians 1:9-10) NLT

Reflection:

- What are some things your heart desires? How does God want you to live your life?

_____

_____

_____

_____

_____

Prayer:

Father,

I pray that you give me spiritual understanding and wisdom so that I can live according to Your will and purpose for my life. I pray that I will bear good fruit and because of it draw people towards You. Thank you for placing the desires inside of my heart and for giving me purpose. Give me the strength to stay on the righteous path and carry out Your will for my life. Because of You, I can live my best life. In Jesus name, Amen.

Affirmations:

o   I will live a life that is pleasing to God.

Don't Settle

Don't settle for the major, don't settle for the career, don't settle for the job, and don't settle for the plan that is not for you. To settle for less is to opt out of the plan that God has for your life. Sometimes we choose this option because we are impatient and can't comprehend how God is working on our behalf. Don't let your emotions and instability deter you from your destiny. They are merely feelings and have nothing to do with what God is doing in your life. Your relationship with God is a faith walk. You may not always be able to see where He is taking you, sometimes your vision will be cloudy. But your faith will assure you that He is taking you places that you would have never imagined (2 Corinthians 5:7).

With that being said, consider the things that God has for you before you make any major decision. Here are some questions you can ask yourself: Is this what God would have for me? Does this align with God's will for my life? Is this the right (fill in the bank) for me? If you don't know the answers to these questions, pray about them. He will lead you to make the right decisions. God knows what is best for you, even when you don't. He has already set the path before you. Keep your mind on the things God has for you and you won't settle for the things that He doesn't.

Meditate on these scriptures:

- ○ "For I know the plans I have for you," declares the Lord, "plans to prosper you and not to harm you, plans to give you hope and a future." (Jeremiah 29:11) NIV
- ○ "Trust in the LORD with all your heart, and do not lean on your own understanding. In all your ways acknowledge him, and he will

make straight your paths." (Proverbs 3:5-6) ESV

- o "Set your minds on things that are above, not on things that are on earth." (Colossians 3:2) ESV

Reflection:

- o How can you keep your mind on the things God has for you?

_____

_____

_____

_____

_____

Prayer:

Father,

Help me to develop a greater trust in You and the plan that You have for my life. I know that You have plans to prosper me and not to harm me. I want to make my decisions always keeping in mind that Your plan and will is perfect. What You have for me, is for me and I will not settle. I pray that I don't let my feelings get in the way of what You are doing in my life. Continue to lead and guide me as I take this faith walk with You. In Jesus name, Amen.

Affirmations :

o   I won't settle for less than God's best.

Day 14

Trust Issues

Trust begins with faith. It is impossible to trust in something you never believed was true or would happen. Your lack of trust may be stemming from your lack of belief. It may be difficult for you to trust in the plan God has for you if you don't believe in yourself. The only way to increase your level of faith is to increase risk in your life. For God to use you the way He wants to use you, you have to trust in Him. Your trust in God will reflect in the relationships you have with other people. If you haven't established a sense of trust and respect towards God, it will be difficult for you to establish these things in other relationships. Your distrust in people can be dangerous at times. It can alter your sense of judgment and cause you to make decisions you will regret.

You need people to help you fulfill your purpose. The right people at the right time will help shift you into the right direction. Your lack of trust in people will cause you to miss key points in your life that required change and action. Surround yourself with people that you can trust. Establish healthy relationships with other believers in Christ. It will change your life forever. God will give you the spirit of discernment to determine who is really on your team and in your corner. Let your faith in God be the foundation for your trust and relationships with other people. God doesn't want you to live a life of isolation, void of people that you can trust. There are people that were placed in your life for a reason. Find those people and build with them (Proverbs 27:17).

Meditate on these scriptures:

- o "And without faith it is impossible to please him, for whoever would draw near to God must believe that he exists and that he rewards those who seek him." (Hebrews 11:6) ESV

o 'Those who know your name trust in you, for you, LORD, have never forsaken those who seek you." (Psalm 9:10) NIV

o "Let us think of ways to motivate one another to acts of love and good works. 25 And let us not neglect our meeting together, as some people do, but encourage one another, especially now that the day of his return is drawing near." (Hebrews 10:24-25) NLT

Reflection :

o How has your lack of trust in God affected your life and relationships?

_____

_____

_____

_____

_____

Prayer:

Father,

I pray that You send the right people in my life at the right time. Send me the people that I can trust and know have my best interest at heart. Thank You for the people that You have already used and are using in my life to motivate me and make me stronger. I speak that my faith and trust in You will increase so that I can have an increase in the connections in my life. I trust in You and what You are trying to do through me and the people in my life. In Jesus name, Amen.

Affirmations :

o   I will trust in the Lord.

Day 15

Wake, Pray, Slay

The best way to conquer your day is to start with the presence of the Lord. How often do we wake up "on the wrong side of the bed" in the morning? This changes the trajectory of our day ahead. For the majority of the day we feel groggy and want to go back to bed. Or, have you ever woken up feeling, refreshed, rejuvenated and ready to start your day? You end up getting a lot more accomplished when you feel this way. In college I found out that I wasn't a morning person. I struggled daily to wake up early for my morning classes. Because of this I always tried to schedule afternoon classes, with the hope that I would be able to get a little extra sleep and start my days with the right mind and attitude. This also gave me more time in the morning to pray, read The Word and listen to worship music.

Listening to worship music and upbeat gospel songs gave me the energy and joy to accomplish my school work and get through the day. Often times I would pray and read later in the day, after I had set the tone for the morning. Because I am not a morning person, I needed something that would give me that extra boost of confidence. With that being said, figure out what works best for you. You will learn a lot about yourself and your habits, good and bad, while in school. Find some music you like that will shift you into the right spirit. Let God fill you with His Word and love so that the rest of your day will be rooted in it. And most importantly thank God for waking you up and for the wonderful day He has planned ahead. Wake up in the morning, seek the presence of God and you will slay your day.

Meditate on these scriptures :

o "This is the day that the Lord has made; let us rejoice and be glad in it." (Psalm 118:24) ESV

- "Let me hear of your unfailing love each morning, for I am trusting you. Show me where to walk, for I give myself to you." (Psalm 143:8) NLT
- "It is because of the Lord's lovingkindnesses that we are not consumed, Because His [tender] compassions never fail. They are new every morning; Great and beyond measure is Your faithfulness." (Lamentations 3:22-23) AMP

Reflection :

- Consider how the start of your day sets the tone for the rest of your day. How can you jumpstart your days by starting with the presence of the Lord?

_____

_____

_____

_____

_____

Prayer:

Father,

Thank you for waking me up this morning and for this beautiful day you have created. I pray that your love, peace, and joy will encompass me throughout the day. Allow me to accomplish all the things that need to be completed with the right, mind, heart and spirit. I pray that you keep me rooted in Your Word and give me the strength to make it through this day and every day. In Jesus name, Amen.

Affirmations :

○ I will start my day seeking the presence of the Lord.

Day 16

In the Midst of the Storm

The storm is only temporary. It may not feel like it. Even if it endures for a long period of time, it WILL NOT last forever. It may not seem like it. You may be looking around at the dark clouds and sky above you, thinking that it will never pass. A thing I learned about the storm is that it is only meant to propel you forward while growing you in the process. A storm can be classified as any type of hardship, obstacle, or challenge you might face while in college. There are some storms that can be prepared for, but there are others that come when you least expect it. Although you may be experiencing strong winds and turbulence, there are three things you can always be sure of: God is with you. God is powerful enough to change any circumstance. And you are going to make it to the other side.

This is similar to what happened to the disciples when they were on the boat with Jesus (Mark 4:35-41). Before they crossed the sea, Jesus told them that they were going to the other side. After the storm appeared and strong waves were crashing onto the boat, they were afraid and began to panic. Meanwhile, Jesus was resting at the back of the boat. They awakened Him with their frustrations and He spoke peace over the atmosphere. The wind and waves obeyed the words of Jesus and peace was still. He then asked the disciples why they were so afraid and where their faith was. Don't let your conditions be the determinant of where God is going to take you. If He is leading you in one direction, don't be surprised when the storm arrives. That wind is going to press you forward into your destiny. The storm has a purpose. It is molding you, shaping you, and teaching you a lesson. If you search for wisdom and understanding in Him, you will find the message in the mess and the strength to endure.

Meditate on these scriptures:

o "But he said to me, "My grace is sufficient for you, for my power is made perfect in weakness." Therefore, I will boast all the more gladly of my weaknesses, so that the power of Christ may rest upon me. For the sake of Christ, then, I am content with weaknesses, insults, hardships, persecutions, and calamities. For when I am weak, then I am strong." (2 Corinthians 12:9-10) ESV

o "More than that, we rejoice in our sufferings, knowing that suffering produces endurance, and endurance produces character, and character produces hope, and hope does not put us to shame, because God's love has been poured into our hearts through the Holy Spirit who has been given to us." (Romans 5:3-5) ESV

Reflection:

- How have the storms in your life shaped you into the person you are today?

Prayer:

Father,

Things may not always look good, but I trust You. I may not always know where You are taking me, but I trust you. I thank you for sending the storm and anything else that would help propel me into my destiny. I pray that my faith will mature as I am learning to trust You through the good, the bad, and the ugly. I will not let my circumstances determine where I am headed and the ways You are working in my life. In Jesus' name, Amen.

Affirmations :

- When I am afraid, I will trust in the Lord.

Day 17

Stress – Relief

How do you typically overcome stressful situations and emotions? Do you respond in healthy or unhealthy ways? Do you find yourself coping with the stress or letting it overtake you? These are all important questions to consider now that you're in college. College can be a stressful time for many people. Finding out the way you deal with stress and the best methods of release will be life changing for you. Many students fall victim to the unnecessary stress of procrastination and exam week. Procrastination may be a tool that some people use to get their work done at the last minute, but stress only makes things worse. If you are invested into your success and college career it is inevitable for you to become stressed at some point. The best thing for you to do is to arm yourself with strategy.

The most stressful time of my college career was during my senior year. I was in the process of finishing my classes while trying to figure out my next steps after graduation. I was so stressed that I wasn't even happy about graduating and what the near future would hold for me. I allowed my emotions to convince myself that I wasn't doing enough. I finally received peace by taking long, intimate walks on a path that was near my apartment. Sometimes I would listen to worship music and other times I would just listen to the sound of nature. I felt refreshed while taking in the sunlight, clearing my mind and enjoying the amazing view. By doing this daily, I produced both peace and joy in my life. Harbor a lifestyle of peace. Take the time to release your mind of all stress, anxiety and worry. As you are reading this, I speak that the peace of God will inhabit in your life and surpass your understanding.

Meditate on these scriptures :

o "Do not be anxious about anything, but in everything by prayer and supplication with thanksgiving let your requests be made known to God. And the peace of God, which surpasses all understanding, will guard your hearts and your minds in Christ Jesus." (Philippians 4:6-7) ESV

o "Peace I leave with you; my peace I give to you. Not as the world gives do I give to you. Let not your hearts be troubled, neither let them be afraid." (John 14:27) ESV

o "Therefore I tell you, do not be anxious about your life, what you will eat or what you will drink, nor about your body, what you will put on. Is not life more than food, and the body more than clothing? Look at the birds of the air: they neither sow nor reap nor gather into barns, and yet your heavenly Father feeds them. Are you not of more value than they?

And which of you by being anxious can add a single hour to his span of life? And why are you anxious about clothing? Consider the lilies of the field, how they grow: they neither toil nor spin, yet I tell you, even Solomon in all his glory was not arrayed like one of these. But if God so clothes the grass of the field, which today is alive and tomorrow is thrown into the oven, will he not much more clothe you," (Matthew 6:25-30) ESV

Reflection:

o   Find a scripture that speaks to you and gives you peace. Write it down and refer to it whenever you are feeling stressed.

_____

_____

_____

_____

_____

Prayer:

Father,

I thank you for Your peace that surpasses all understanding. I pray that Your peace will outweigh my doubt, stress, anxiety, worry and insecurity. I pray that I am secure in You and Your guidance. I thank you for replacing my burdens with Your unconditional love and care. Thank you for always keeping me in mind. I do not have to worry because You are always providing for me. In Jesus' name, Amen.

Affirmations :

o   I speak peace over my life and mind.

Day 18

"Late Nights & Early Mornings"

While in college I had my fair share of late nights and early mornings. There were plenty of times I stayed up past 3AM knowing that I had to be up early in the morning. There will be some nights that you have to stay up past your usual bedtime to study or some mornings you have to wake up earlier than usual. Other nights you might have to pull an all-nighter. There may even be some nights that you decide to hang out instead of studying for your exam or completing your project that's due the next week. It's life and it happens, just don't make a habit out of those things. Think smarter, not harder and save yourself the trouble of cramming.

As you are spending the majority of your time in class, studying, working, and hanging out with friends, don't forget about your rest. If you want to actually remember everything you studied and not become distracted by sleep deprivation, I suggest you get a decent amount of sleep. The combination of stress and not getting enough sleep can be dangerous for college students. It can lead you into depression, anxiety and drain you spiritually. Create some time in your schedule for restoration and debriefing. Restoration is good for your mind and body, and it creates balance. Figure out the times of the day that are best for you to study and get things done. People operate differently at different times of the day. I prefer to get most of my work done during the day, so I can have free time at night. College is all about strategy. Find the right strategy and implement it to the best of your ability. Rest paired with hard work is the recipe for success.

Meditate on these scriptures:

- "Then Jesus said, "Come to me, all of you who are weary and carry heavy burdens, and I will give you rest. Take my yoke upon you. Let me teach you, because I am humble and gentle at heart, and you will find rest for your souls. For my yoke is easy to bear, and the burden I give you is light." (Matthew 11:28:30) NLT

- "So also faith by itself, if it does not have works, is dead." (James 2:17) ESV

Reflection :

- Are you a morning or night person? How does your sleep schedule affect your energy and work ethic?

_____

_____

_____

_____

_____

Prayer:

Father,

Thank you for giving me rest. I pray that I develop positive study and work habits that allow me to get the proper rest I need to be a good student. Help me to align the right strategies that will work for me instead of against me. I understand the importance of rest on my mental health. Send the right people that will help keep me accountable. In Jesus' name, Amen.

Affirmations :

o   I will restore my mind and body through rest.

Day 19

Heart Checks

What are your intentions? As I touched on in the introduction, there was a period of time while I was writing this devotional that I lost my focus. My original intent was to help other women that may be struggling like I was to find solace in the identity I knew nothing about. Yet somewhere along the process I allowed my feelings and emotions to dictate my actions. I allowed my mind-state and situation to deter what I knew about this devotional, that it would shift and break things. I was coming from the right place, while I wasn't in the right space. Had I forgotten my original intent? There I was needing a shift and a breakthrough to finish what I had started. Had I forgotten about the many young women that inspired me to write this devotional? I had to do a heart check.

A heart check is when you have to consider what your mind, will and emotions are telling you versus what God has already said. Understand this, I am not saying that your feelings aren't validated, but there will be many times you have to push pass them to accomplish your goals and press towards the finish line. As a student you have to consistently meet deadlines for assignments. There needs to be a balance that doesn't allow stress, fatigue, laziness, etc. prevent you from being studious. Take a break. Be honest with yourself about the way you are feeling. Put it all out there on the table. Let there be a release so that a renewal can't take place. Then get back to work. Continue to fill your mind and heart with the promises and fulfillment of God. Speak those things that are not, until they are becoming and have become your truth (Mark 11:24).

Meditate on these scriptures:

- The heart is deceitful above all things, and desperately sick; who can understand it? "I the Lord search the heart and test the mind, to give every man according to his ways, according to the fruit of his deeds." (Jeremiah 17:9-10) ESV

- Create in me a clean heart, O God, and renew a right spirit within me. (Psalm 51:10) ESV

- Above all else, guard your heart, for everything you do flows from it. (Proverbs 4:23) NIV

Reflection :

- Why would God call the heart deceitful? Give yourself a heart check and be honest. What state is your heart in?

_____

_____

_____

_____

_____

Prayer:

Father,

Create me a clean heart, a heart that is truthful, selfless, and loving. Strengthen my ability to discern my emotions and protect my heart. I pray that my heart is aligned with your spirit and that I am able to accomplish all that needs to be done. If there is any negative intention, way or motive inside of my heart, I pray that you replace it with love, grace, and humility. In Jesus' name, Amen.

Affirmations :

o   I will guard my heart with love.

Day 20

Forgiveness

Forgiveness is the gateway to true freedom. Jesus died so that we could be granted forgiveness for ourselves AND one another. When I first came to college, I was carrying a lot of bitterness from relationships and experiences in my life. I was so excited about going to college in the mountains of Blacksburg, far from everything and everyone that I knew. I was longing for a fresh start, an escape. I was happy to start the new chapter in my life, but I was unhappy. It wasn't until I truly embraced forgiveness, that I felt free. Your unwillingness to forgive has a deeper effect on your mind and state of being than you realize. It brings forth a heaviness on your spirit. The weight you carry affects every single area of your life, whether it be your relationships with people, your school-work, your self-confidence, your motivation or your work ethic. Don't allow people and things from your past to keep you off your game. You are in college for a reason. God is using this time in your life to instill a greater understanding of purpose inside of you.

I challenge you today to embrace forgiveness and to let go of all bitterness, including the negative feelings you have towards yourself. Sometimes we are the hardest person for us to forgive. Don't allow you to get in the way of your own growth and what God is doing in your life. Forgiveness may not be easy, but ask yourself is the dead weight you're carrying worth it? Is it worth the hurt and pain bottled-up inside of you? Is it worth the constant feeling of heaviness? Freedom is your portion. Forgiveness is your portion. Choose love instead of hate. Guard your heart and your mind. Be free and walk in your freedom. It belongs to you! During today's prayer speak aloud all of the people and situations you forgive. Name them one by one and be specific, even if it seems small. After you speak them, release them and hold on to them no more. My prayer is that as you lay each of these things down, you will be freed and comforted by the love of God.

Meditate on these scriptures:

- "If we confess our sins, he is faithful and just to forgive us our sins and to cleanse us from all unrighteousness." (1 John 1:9) ESV
- "Get rid of all bitterness, rage, anger, harsh words, and slander, as well as all types of evil behavior. Instead, be kind to each other, tenderhearted, forgiving one another, just as God through Christ has forgiven you." (Ephesians 4:31-32) NLT
- "If you forgive those who sin against you, your heavenly Father will forgive you. But if you refuse to forgive others, your Father will not forgive your sins." (Matthew 6:14-15) NLT

Reflection :

○ How can your unwillingness to forgive have the power to keep you in a place of bondage?

_____

_____

_____

_____

_____

Prayer:

Father,

Forgive me for my sins and forgive those that have sinned against me. Help me to forgive myself and others the way that You forgive us. I no longer want to be unforgiving, nor harbor any bitterness and heaviness in my spirit. Free me from the hurt and sin of my past and allow me to walk in wholeness. I speak against depression, bitterness, and feelings of unworthiness. Thank You for the ultimate sacrifice, Jesus, who paid the price for me. (DECLARE FORGIVENESS) In Jesus' name, Amen.

Affirmations :

o I will forgive because I have been forgiven.

Day 21

Filling the Void

As I write this chapter, the song "Nobody Greater" by VaShawn Mitchell is echoing in my spirit: "I searched all over couldn't find nobody. I looked high and low, still couldn't find nobody. Nobody greater, nobody greater, no nobody greater than You". Are you searching high and low for something or someone to fill the void in your heart? Are you constantly searching and searching only to find yourself back where you started? As much as you are searching for yourself and your purpose, God is chasing after you. By nature, you were designed to live in harmony with Him. He created you to need Him. It is a part of your innate ability to worship God. All of you needs all of Him, and all of Him wants all of you. Christ not only wants to fill you; but fill you to overflow and outpour. What does that mean? Even the people connected to you are going to be blessed. You are going to leave a Godly remnant everywhere you go because His glory shines through you.

Fill those places that were once occupied with hurt, pain, and lack of purpose with the fulfillment of Christ. You are no longer bound by those things. You are called to walk in the understanding of who God is and who you are. The more you seek Him, the more you will find yourself. The more you fill yourself with His Word, the more wisdom. understanding, and grace you will have. Don't let anyone take from you, what they didn't give you. You have the spirit of God inside of you. You are wired to be victorious, overcome and live abundantly.

Meditate on these scriptures:

o "As a deer pants for flowing streams, so pants my soul for you, O God. My soul thirsts for God, for the living God. When shall I come and appear before God?" (Psalm 42:1-2) ESV

- "Jesus answered, "Everyone who drinks this water will be thirsty again, but whoever drinks the water I give them will never thirst. Indeed, the water I give them will become in them a spring of water welling up to eternal life"." (John 4:13-14) NIV
- "I am the vine; you are the branches. If you remain in me and I in you, you will bear much fruit; apart from me you can do nothing." (John 15:5) NIV

Reflection:

- Is there a void in your life that needs to be filled by Christ?

Prayer:

Father,

I pray that you reveal and fill every void in my life. Increase my hunger to seek Your face and Your Word. Keep me in perfect peace as I continue to press towards You. Fill me with Your glory, grace and mercy. I speak against any attack that would come against the love and freedom You have given me. In Jesus' name, Amen.

Affirmations:

- I am fulfilled through Christ.

Day 22

Me – Time

Some of my most freeing moments in college were moments that I spent in my room in solitude. They were moments of reflection, prayer, relaxation, meditation, peace, dancing and sometimes loud music. As women we tend to dedicate much of our time and energy towards other people. We have to learn how to pour as much into ourselves as we do to our friends and family. This starts with "me-time", having time set aside for you to be you. Most of your time in college is spent in a social environment, whether it be your classes, a study group, club meetings, hanging out with friends, etc. You will grow to appreciate the time you do have by yourself, especially if you have roommates. Cherish the time that you have alone with yourself and God. And, if you feel like that time isn't enough, find some more.

Pouring into yourself means devoting more time to God, practicing more of the things that you love, and focusing more on your happiness and your dreams. We've all heard the saying: "People make time for what is important to them". Your spiritual, mental, emotional, and physical state should be a priority in your life. Your future should be a priority in your life. You will not regret placing your energy and attention towards working on yourself. You are on the journey to becoming a better and happier you. Therefore, you don't have any time to waste. Be strategic with your time and honest about what you need. People often say "Life isn't about you" when referring to the way we should spend our time, but I disagree. Life is about you: your freedom, your peace, your fulfillment and your joy. Christ died for you to have those things, AND life more abundantly (John 10:10 KJV).

Meditate on these scriptures:

- "But when you pray, go into your room and shut the door and pray to your Father who is in secret. And your Father who sees in secret will reward you." (Matthew 6:6) ESV

- "I came so they can have real and eternal life, more and better life than they ever dreamed of." (John 10:10) MSG

Reflection:

- What are some ways you can implement more me-time in your schedule?

_____

_____

_____

_____

_____

Prayer:

Father,

I am grateful for the time that we spend together. I pray that it is filled with joy and serenity. Thank you for instilling the passions and the deep desires in my heart. Help me to dedicate as much time to myself as I do to others. I want to be more diligent with the time that you have given me. Ignite a fire inside of me to pursue my purpose like never before. In Jesus' name, Amen.

Affirmations:

○ I will love myself first.

Day 23

Expectations

God is able. Able to exceed your expectations. Able to bring you out of those dry places. Able to renew your mind and shift your thinking. Able to give you the blueprint to the master plan. Able to set you up in the right place at the right time. Sometimes we have to remind ourselves that God is able. Things change, people change, seasons change, but God remains the same (Hebrews 13:8). You can count on Him to show up. You can count on him in the face of adversity. He is The Promise Keeper and The Way Maker. He is The Healer and the Miracle Worker. Walk in a state of expectancy concerning what God is about to do in your life. As a believer in Christ, this is the posture God expects and desires from you.

God's word says that He "has not given us a spirit of fear, but of power and of love and of a sound mind" (2 Timothy 1:7). How powerful is that! What is God really saying to us? He gave us resurrection power to bring dead things to life, unconditional love that covers a multitude of sins, and a mind that is competent, in good condition and financially secure. Fear isn't your portion, neither is worry or stress. Position your mind in expectancy. You have the capacity to stand firm and faithful, even in the toughest of times. God will cover you. He will provide the finances for you to finish school. You will see your dreams and visions come into fruition. His plans for you are great and magnificent. Don't believe anything less than the truth and less than His Word. He will never leave you, nor will He ever forsake you.

Meditate on these scriptures:

o "Now to Him who is able to [carry out His purpose and] do superabundantly more than all that we dare ask or think [infinitely beyond our greatest prayers, hopes, or dreams], according to His power that is at work within us," (Ephesians 3:20) AMP

o "No eye has seen, no ear has heard, and no mind has imagined what God has prepared for those who love him." But it was to us that God revealed these things by his Spirit. For his Spirit searches out everything and shows us God's deep secrets." (1 Corinthians 2:9-19) NLT

o "Ask, and it will be given to you; seek, and you will find; knock, and it will be opened to you." (Matthew 7:7) ESV

Reflection :

o How can you align your expectations with God's plan for your life?

_____

_____

_____

_____

_____

Prayer:

Father,

I thank you for the calling you placed on my life. I thank you for the plans you established for me before the beginning of time. I thank you for positioning me in expectancy for Your Glory to be revealed. Thank you for being The Way Maker and The Promise Keeper. I will forever trust in you, In Jesus' name, Amen.

Affirmations:

o God is able.

Day 24

Real Friends

In college I learned many valuable lessons about friendship. The friendships you are forming now have the capability to grow into something life-long and beautiful. Soon my college best friend and I will share the same last name. WOW. This is the perfect time for you to meet new people and make new connections. You never know who you'll meet in college that you may be connected to years from now. Your colleagues may become your future business partners, the Godparents of your children, or in my case the love of your life. Step out of your comfort zone and don't limit your interactions to certain people. Be strategic with the friendships and connections you make while in college. You can expand your sphere of influence by expanding your knowledge and network. God's desire is for you to build genuine relationships with His people.

People can only have as much access to your life as you allow them. Allow the right people access, those that God has called you to. The people you surround yourself with have a direct influence on your character and growth. Therefore, you should surround yourself with like-minded individuals. "Birds of a feather flock together," so flock with the people that can see the purpose and vision waiting to be birthed inside of you. Flock with the people that are invested in your future. Flock with those that build you up, instead of tearing you down. They are your real friends. Don't waste your time in meaningless relationships. Sever the ties if you need to but do it in love. Do it for you! God will restore your lost friendships. He will make room for the right people.

Meditate on these scriptures:

o "Do not be deceived: "Bad company ruins good morals."" (1 Corinthians 15:33) ESV

o "Walk with the wise and become wise, for a companion of fools suffers harm." (Proverbs 13:20) NIV

o "Two people are better off than one, for they can help each other succeed. If one person falls, the other can reach out and help. But someone who falls alone is in real trouble." (Ecclesiastes 4:9-10) NLT

Reflection:

o Are there any relationships that God has been telling you to let go? What does true friendship look like to you?

_____

_____

_____

_____

_____

Prayer:

Father,

I pray that you reveal my real friends to me. Give me the discernment and strength to cut off the negative relationships in my life. Send the right people that should be a part of my life. Send those that are connected to my future and destiny. Teach me Your ways so that I can become a more loyal and dependable friend. I am grateful for the people you have blessed me with and assigned to my life. In Jesus' name, Amen.

Affirmations:

o   I deserve true friendship.

Day 25

Wildflower

"In a field of roses, she is a wildflower." -Unknown

I decided to begin this devotional with one of my favorite quotes. I love this quote because it reminds me a lot of myself. It parallels my personality and nature as a woman. This quote was a part of the inspiration behind me writing this devotional. It helped me redefine the definition of wild. A wildflower is an exotic and rare plant. They thrive among other plant species and grow in some of the wildest conditions. To be a wildflower is to be set apart. You are in this world, not of it. You are called to be set apart. You are called to be a leader, not a follower. You are called to set an example for other believers and people in the world. You were not designed to fit in with the crowd. Stop trying to fit in, when you were called to stand out. The quicker you accept this truth about yourself, the greater understanding you will have of your identity.

What does it mean to be set apart? It means that your characteristics distinguish you from other people. There is something special and unique about you that no one else can offer. It's the wonderful thing about being you, only you can do that. Stay true to yourself while in college, and don't let people who don't know themselves tell you who and what you're not. It's one of the biggest mistakes you could make. Remain true to your passions and aspirations. Stay grounded in your beliefs and values. Don't compromise your morals. Choose to accept your true identity over a false one. You are a wildflower, you bloom despite what is going on around you. Stand tall and beautiful. You are the light in the darkness. You can not be dimmed. Don't run from it, simply shine.

Meditate on these scriptures:

o "You have been set apart as holy to the Lord your God, and he has chosen you from all the nations of the earth to be his own special treasure." (Deuteronomy 14:2) NLT

o "You are the light of the world. A city set on a hill cannot be hidden. Nor do people light a lamp and put it under a basket, but on a stand, and it gives light to all in the house. In the same way, let your light shine before others, so that they may see your good works and give glory to your Father who is in heaven." (Matthew 5:14-16) ESV

Reflection:

o Throughout your life, how has God set you apart?

_____

_____

_____

_____

_____

Prayer:

Father,

Thank You for setting me apart and creating me for Your unique purpose. Give me the heart to be a better leader and example for Your people. I pray that You reveal more about my identity and the depth of the calling on my life. Keep me grounded and rooted in the truth of Your Word. I pray that I stay true to myself and the woman you created me to be. In Jesus' name, Amen.

Affirmations:

○ I am a wildflower.

Day 26

Greater Works

Greater are the works that you were called to do. Did you know that the works God established for your life were greater than the works Jesus accomplished while on this Earth (John 14:12)? Jesus said it Himself. If that doesn't spark something inside of you, I don't know what will. It definitely sparked something inside of me. Even as I am writing this, I am receiving a greater revelation of identity and excitement about what is to come. Allow heaven to download into you at this moment. Open your ears and heart to what God is longing to reveal to you. Let Him speak life and purpose inside of you. The Lord says, "Come unto Me and I will show you greater."

Yes, you are just THAT powerful. You have the breath of the living God inside of you. It's time for you to recognize the authority that you carry and to start implementing it on your campus, in your classes, and among your peers. I took a philosophy class my senior year entitled "Knowledge and Reality." The class was largely about spirituality and whether or not God exists. I recognized how God wanted to use me as a beacon of light and mouthpiece in my classroom. There were often times I spoke about the nature of God and God-given purpose during our discussions. As I began to declare the word of God, other classmates that were believers in Christ did the same. One day the Holy Spirit prompted me to leave a Daily Bread book on the desk of one of my classmates, who happened to be a non-believer. I considered a million ways I could go around this task, but finally I made the decision to move. My heart was beating extremely fast and I was nervous, but I eventually did it. I chose to walk in the authority that God gave me and be obedient to what the Holy Spirit wanted me to do. That may have been the closest my classmate had ever been to the Word of God. God wants to use you in that same manner to bring forth change on your campus, to be a voice of truth to your classmates, and to walk in love and light towards those who are lost. Greater works are to come.

Meditate on these scriptures:

o "Truly, truly, I say to you, whoever believes in me will also do the works that I do; and greater works than these will he do, because I am going to the Father." (John 14:12) ESV

o "Little children, you are from God and have overcome them, for he who is in you is greater than he who is in the world." (1 John 4:4) ESV

o "But someone will say, "You have faith and I have works." Show me your faith apart from your works, and I will show you my faith by my works." (James 2:18) ESV

Reflection:

o Consider all of the works Jesus did while on this Earth. What does it mean for you to do that and more?

_____

_____

_____

_____

_____

Prayer:

Father,

I thank you for speaking life and purpose inside of me. I pray that you use me in a mighty way on my campus to spread the gospel and Your Word. I thank you for identity and the greater works I am to fulfill in the Earth. Give me the boldness and confidence to walk in the authority you have given me. I want to remain in tune and be submissive to the Holy Spirit. In Jesus' name, Amen.

Affirmations:

- Greater is in me.
- I will fulfill great works.

Day 27

Doubting the Call

"Have I not commanded you? Be strong and courageous. Do not be frightened, and do not be dismayed, for the LORD your God is with you wherever you go." (Joshua 1:9)

I must admit, it may seem easier to doubt all of what you know to be true, rather than to accept it. There have been plenty of times that I have encountered fear and doubt, even while writing this devotional. It was easier to me to procrastinate and set aside writing than it was for me to get focused and see it through. It was easier for me to doubt my competence to publish a book than it was for me trust in the vision God gave me. If I had let fear and doubt consume me, I wouldn't have been able to touch the many lives God intended for me to touch through this devotional. Those alternatives were easy, but they weren't beneficial. They weren't impactful to the Kingdom of God. Your decision to accept the call on your life carries weight. It's not just about you. There are people connected to your purpose.

Don't give fear and doubt the power to interfere with God's plan for your life. You didn't come this far to give up on your dreams. You didn't come this far to forsake your purpose. It is only evidence that what God is doing your life is groundbreaking. This wouldn't be a faith walk if you didn't have to fully rely on God, despite your circumstances and despite your capabilities. You were destined for this. You were purposed for this. Don't let one thought of complacency become your reality, and don't believe the lies of the enemy. Take that fear and turn it into a consuming fire. A consuming fire that burns with the passion to do the will of God. Take that doubt and transform it into the desire to seek God with all of your heart.

Meditate on these scriptures:

- Fear not, for I am with you; be not dismayed, for I am your God; I will strengthen you, I will help you, I will uphold you with my righteous right hand. (Isaiah 41:10) ESV
- "She is clothed with strength and dignity, and she laughs without fear of the future." (Proverbs 31:25) NLT
- "God is within her, she will not fall;" (Psalm 45:6) NIV

Reflection:

- How can you consistently feed your faith to starve your doubts?

_____

_____

_____

_____

_____

Prayer:

Father,

I pray that you cleanse me of every bit of fear, worry and doubt that is trying to consume me. I trust in You and the purpose that You have for my life. Light a fire inside of me to do Your Will and a desire to seek You with my whole heart. Purify my heart Lord and my intentions. I pray that I walk with You every step of the way and my eyes are stayed on you. In Jesus' name, Amen.

Affirmations:

- o   God is with me, I will not fear.
- o   I will walk in my calling.

Day 28

Qualified

If no one ever told you this, you are qualified. The moment God spoke life into you, you were qualified. The moment He thought you into existence, you were qualified. Your past does not disqualify you from God's love. Your mess-ups won't change God's mind about His plan for your life. You are who He said you are. He sees you in a different lens because His ways and thoughts are higher than ours (Isaiah 55:8-9). He knows you as His daughter and you are precious to His sight. God calls those who the world deems as unqualified. He is the one who turns death into life and open the eyes of the blind. Open your eyes to the perspective God has of you and understand that a higher level of thinking is required for you to accept His call. If you are wondering why, it's because He loves you. It's because of His grace and mercy (Ephesians 2:8-9).

You are affirmed by Christ. Therefore, you cannot totally be rejected by man. Don't let thoughts of inadequacy trap you into a vicious cycle of rejection and identity crisis. Use the Word of God and the authority God has given you to war over those thoughts. Speak life over yourself and your circumstance. Rejection does not belong to you, nor was it ever intended for you. God gave you a name and a purpose. He accepted and established a place for you in the Kingdom. When your heart is set on living your life for Christ, there is going to be a lot of background noise. Learn how to tune out all of the noise while intensifying God's voice in your ear. He wants to develop a greater sense of clarity and direction inside of you. Keep your mind and heart guarded from the tricks of the enemy. You are great enough. You are the chosen ones.

Meditate on these scriptures:

- "But you are a chosen race, a royal priesthood, a holy nation, a people for his own possession, that you may proclaim the excellencies of him who called you out of darkness into his marvelous light." (1 Peter 2:9) ESV

- "You did not choose me, but I chose you and appointed you that you should go and bear fruit and that your fruit should abide, so that whatever you ask the Father in my name, he may give it to you." (John 15:16) ESV

- "And those whom he predestined he also called, and those whom he called he also justified, and those whom he justified he also glorified." (Romans 8:30) ESV

Reflection:

- Find a scripture that ministers to you about being chosen by God. Keep it close to your heart.

_____

_____

_____

_____

_____

Prayer:

Father,

Thank you for choosing me. Thank you for giving me a name and a purpose. Thank you for calling me out of the darkness and into your light. I am forever grateful. Purify my heart from the rejection I have been carrying from my past. I want to be whole and complete in You. Through your grace and love I am qualified and able to stand. In Jesus' name, Amen.

Affirmations:

o   I am no longer bound by rejection, fear and doubt.

o   I am loved. I am qualified. I am accepted.

Day 29

Unapologetic

Being unapologetic is your willingness to stand firm in who God created you to be. It doesn't always have to be communicated to the people around you. It is reflected inside of you and through you. Don't waste your time explaining yourself to people who don't want to understand you. Everyone isn't going to accept you for who you are and that's okay. Those are not your people. There will be people that are attracted to your confidence and boldness in Christ. People that see the vision God placed in your heart. Don't stand around waiting for others to recognize you. God sees you. He saw you before you saw yourself. He is watching you sow seeds of love and kindness into His Kingdom. The goal was to never seek validation from people. It was to first seek the Kingdom and His righteousness.

You have already been given the permission and the authority, the keys and the blueprint to your future. You may not have every piece to the puzzle but through faith you will receive all that God has for you. Now is the time for new beginnings. Start that women's group, start that organization, start that business, start those applications. Whatever it is that God has placed in your heart, it won't be fulfilled until you become diligent with it. It's time for you to walk unashamed and unapologetic in your purpose. It's time for you to walk in love and grace. It's time for you to walk with your head held high. Get in the position to receive the outpour God has for you, and don't apologize for it. Remain humble and giving in all that you do, and all that God has given you. Women of God support and uplift each other in confidence and in humility.

Meditate on these scriptures:

o "The Lord is my light and my salvation; whom shall I fear? The Lord is the stronghold of my life; of whom shall I be afraid?" (Psalm 27:1) ESV

o "For I am not ashamed of the gospel, for it is the power of God for salvation to everyone who believes," (Romans 1:16) ESV

o The Great Commission: "And Jesus came and said to them, "All authority in heaven and on earth has been given to me. Go therefore and make disciples of all nations, baptizing them in the name of the Father and of the Son and of the Holy Spirit, teaching them to observe all that I have commanded you. And behold, I am with you always, to the end of the age"." (Matthew 28:18-20) ESV

Reflection:

o How can you be unapologetic in your walk with Christ but still remain humble?

_____

_____

_____

_____

_____

Prayer:

Father,

I pray that I walk more confidently and boldly in the calling you have graced on my life. Thank You for allowing me to come before Your throne and share the gospel unashamed. I desire to be most diligent with the gifts, passions, and resources You have given me. Encourage me with the strength and the motivation to start now and never look back. I will walk unapologetically and in perfect peace. In Jesus' name, Amen.

Affirmations:

o   I am unashamed of the gospel.

Mirror Image

You were created in the image and likeness of God. The definition of likeness is to be alike, a portrait, or representation. You were placed on this Earth to exemplify the character of God, to be fruitful and multiply (Genesis 1:28). Your fruitfulness is what you are sowing into the Kingdom of God and other people's lives. As Christians we are supposed to bear good fruit. Your fruit is your service towards God and mankind. In what ways are you being impactful and influential to someone else? You are a child of God and it is your duty to demonstrate the love of Christ. It is by our fruits that people know who we belong to. When people see you, they should see the God inside of you. There should be something uncommon about what you carry. Your spirit should draw people unto God (John 12:32).

Perception is important. People knew Jesus was the Son of God, because of the life he lived. He walked in authority, power, love, humility and obedience. The same applies to us. We as Christians will never be able to display the true nature of God until we start developing a relationship with the Holy Spirit. The Holy Spirit teaches us the ways of God. It is through our relationship with the Holy Spirit that our character is transformed, and we display the fruits of the spirit. Developing fruit takes time and is definitely a process. A seed doesn't yield fruit the next day. Learn to trust and appreciate your journey as you are learning and growing each day. All God desires is a willing vessel. Your relationship with God is a daily walk. Just keep pressing forward in faith.

Meditate on these scriptures:

o "Then God said, "Let us make man in our image, after our likeness. And let them have dominion over the fish of the sea and over the birds of the heavens and over the livestock and over all the earth and over every creeping thing that creeps on the earth." So God created man in his own image, in the image of God he created him; male and female he created them." (Genesis 1:26-27) ESV

o "But the fruit of the Spirit is love, joy, peace, patience, kindness, goodness, faithfulness, gentleness, self-control; against such things there is no law." (Galatians 5:22-23) ESV

o "A good tree cannot bear bad fruit, and a bad tree cannot bear good fruit. Every tree that does not bear good fruit is cut down and thrown into the fire. Thus, by their fruit you will recognize them." (Matthew 7:18-20) NIV

Reflection:

o How can you, as a believer in Christ, reflect the spirit of God inside of you?

_____

_____

_____

_____

_____

Prayer:

Father,

Thank you for creating me in Your image and likeness. I pray that I am transformed by the power of Your spirit. Establish a new thing inside me. Stir up the purpose and calling within me. Encompass me with the fruits of Your spirit and cultivate the gifts inside of me. I pray that as I lift up your name, people will be drawn unto You. In Jesus' name, Amen.

Affirmations:

o   I am made in the image and likeness of God.
o   I will be fruitful and multiply.

Young, Wild & Free

We finally made it to Day 31. What a journey. My prayer is that you have received something from this, that something has changed inside of you, something has sparked inside of you. I pray that you've found a true freedom and hope. I pray that you've developed a greater sense of self and identity. I pray that you've chosen to walk in the calling and purpose that God destined for your life. I pray that your relationship with God will never be the same. I pray that God has spoken to you through dreams, signs and visions. I pray that you have been fulfilled in Christ.

I pray that you've learned to love yourself and make your happiness a priority. I pray that you've found love, joy peace, kindness, goodness, patience, faithfulness, gentleness and self-control. I pray that you've acquired a hunger to seek the Kingdom of God. I pray that you've found forgiveness and reconciliation in your relationships. I pray that God has given you wisdom, knowledge and understanding. I pray that you will stand strong in the face of trials, tribulations and adversity. I pray that you will trust God, even in the midst of the storm.

I pray that you will touch the lives on your campus. I pray that you will be a light to your friends, family and colleagues. I pray that you will embrace your college years. I pray that you make new relationships with other believers in Christ. I pray that you'll stay focused, be diligent and work hard. I pray that you get involved in your community and serve. I pray that you will keep moving forward and never look back. I pray that your dreams and aspirations will come into fruition. I pray that God keeps you. I pray that you live your life with no regrets. And most of all, I pray that you'll live young, wild and free.

Meditate on these scriptures:

- "For I am about to do something new. See, I have already begun! Do you not see it? I will make a pathway through the wilderness. I will create rivers in the dry wasteland." (Isaiah 43:19) NLT
- "Blessed is she who has believed that the Lord would fulfill his promises to her!" (Luke 1:45) NIV

Reflection:

- In what ways have you grown since you started reading this devotional? What has God revealed to you?

_____

_____

_____

_____

_____

Prayer:

Father,

I couldn't be more thankful for You taking me on this journey. I seal every prayer and word of affirmation spoken over me in this devotional and count it done. This is the start of something new. In Jesus' name, Amen.

Affirmations:

o   I am young, wild and free.

Dear Family,

First, I want to thank my BFF and soon to be husband Maurice, author of *Desperate for Change: 31 Devotionals for College Men Changing Bad Habits Into Winning Decisions,* for constantly pushing and motivating me to work hard and follow my dreams.

I am thankful for my family for their prayers and support in raising me to become the woman I am today, especially my mom for her countless sacrifices and love for me.

I also want to honor the spiritual leaders and men and women of God that have poured into me, helped me grow spiritually and taught me to seek God for myself.

I want to give a special thanks to Dr. Tony Warrick, best-selling author of *Jesus and Coffee: 31 Devotions to Kick-start Your Day*, for being a trailblazer and great mentor.

Thank you to my amazing high-school teacher, Emily Stains, for her encouragement and editing throughout this process; as well as my good friend Xavier for the beautiful cover design.

Lastly, I want to give a shout out and thank you to my social media family for their continued love and support.

To all of my friends and everyone who has been a part of my journey; you are amazing, and I couldn't thank you enough.

Love, Apris

About Apris

Apris is a multi-talented and gifted young woman, brand ambassador, social media influencer and entrepreneur from Richmond, Virginia. She graduated from Virginia Tech in 2018 with a bachelor's degree in Psychology and a minor in Entrepreneurship. Her heart's desire is to be a positive light to young women, especially through social media and entertainment. She began acting and modeling when she was first introduced to the talent ministry Actors, Models & Talent for Christ. She is the founder of The Young Wild and Free Movement, a movement dedicated to inspiring young women to "live their best lives" through serving God and being their true selves.

Her college years were the time God began to reveal her much of her identity, calling and purpose to her. Since then she's been on a life changing journey with God and is continuously taking steps in the direction of her purpose and God's plan for her life. Her devotions are strategic in helping young women that are seeking God and their purpose find the beauty and freedom in growth, transformation and simply being who God created them to be.

Stay Connected!

Follow Apris on Twitter, Instagram & Firework: **@aboutapris**